FLY, YOU STUPID KITE, FLY!

Copr. © 1950, 1952 United Feature Syndicate, Inc.

Peanuts® Parade Paperbacks

FLY, YOU STUPID KITE, FLY!

Cartoons from *You're Out of Your Mind, Charlie Brown!*
and *But We Love You, Charlie Brown*

by Charles M. Schulz

Holt, Rinehart and Winston / New York

Published simultaneously in Canada by Holt, Rinehart
and Winston of Canada, Limited.

First published in this form in 1976.

Library of Congress Catalog Card Number: 76-8673

ISBN: 0-03-018106-2

Printed in the United States of America

10 9 8 7 6 5 4 3 2 1

Copr. © 1950 United Feature Syndicate, Inc.

SCHULZ

WHAM!

SCHULZ

SCHROEDER, I'VE BEEN THINKING...

WHAT IF YOU AND I WERE TO GET MARRIED SOMEDAY, AND HAVE A LOT OF CHILDREN?

AND WHAT IF, INSTEAD OF BEING REAL RICH, WE WERE REAL POOR BECAUSE YOU INSISTED ON PLAYING THE PIANO IN SOME CHEAP LITTLE..

WHAT?

⁑ WHEW ⁑

EVERY NOW AND THEN I THINK MAYBE I SHOULD MARRY AN ACCORDION PLAYER!

SCHULZ

MY MOTHER DIDN'T RAISE ME TO SPEND MY WHOLE LIFE CHASING STICKS!

SCHULZ

CLOMP!

MAY I HELP YOU WITH YOUR PUZZLE, LUCY?

NO! BESIDES, I'M ALMOST DONE..

PLEASE?

OH, GOOD GRIEF! **ALL RIGHT!** HERE...YOU CAN PUT IN THE LAST PIECE..

GOOD! NOW, LET ME SEE.. HOW DOES IT GO? DOES IT FIT LIKE THIS, OR DOES IT FIT LIKE THIS? OR MAYBE DOES IT FIT THIS WAY? LET'S SEE NOW...

DOES IT FIT THIS WAY OR THIS WAY OR THIS WAY? OR MAYBE DOES IT FIT THAT WAY?

MAYBE IT FITS LIKE THIS OR AROUND THIS WAY OR MAYBE IT FITS THIS WAY OR LIKE THIS OR MAYBE..

GIMME THAT PIECE!!

SHE NEVER LETS ME HELP WITH ANYTHING..

SCHULZ

HEY! WHAT'RE Y'DOING THERE?!! WHAT'RE Y'DOING WITH THOSE PLIERS? HEY!

YER **OUT!**

YOU AND THAT STUPID BLANKET!

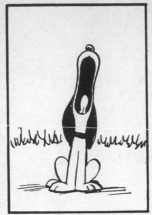

YOU DRIVE ME CRAZY!

LINUS IS ALWAYS WRITING SOMETHING IN THE AIR..

SOMETIMES HE WRITES, SOMETIMES HE DRAWS, SOMETIMES HE JUST SKETCHES...

EVERY NOW AND THEN HE LIKES TO DO A **MURAL**!

SCHULZ

BOY, HOW THAT GIRL CAN DANCE! SHE'S REALLY A BALL OF FIRE! YES, SIR! SHE'S QUITE A GIRL!!

TOO BAD SHE ISN'T A DOG..

SCHULZ

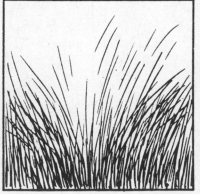

CLOMP!

AAUGH!

NO MANAGER IN THE HISTORY OF BASEBALL HAS EVER HAD TO GO THROUGH WHAT I HAVE TO GO THROUGH!

SCHULZ

I'LL BET I WOULD HAVE MADE A GOOD BALD EAGLE!

SCHULZ

I'M SCARED TO PLAY ANY MORE, CHARLIE BROWN..

THERE'S A VULTURE SITTING ON THE CROQUET STAKE..

A VULTURE?

SCHULZ

OH, GOOD GRIEF!

MY DAD HAS A BETTER UNDERSTANDING OF FOREIGN POLICY THAN YOUR DAD..

OH, GOOD GRIEF!

SCHULZ

I WONDER IF BEETHOVEN WOULD HAVE LIKED ME?

HE DIDN'T LIKE VERY MANY PEOPLE, YOU KNOW..

OH, I'M SURE HE WOULD HAVE LIKED YOU, SCHROEDER...

DO YOU REALLY THINK SO?

SURE

BUT I'LL BET HE WOULD HAVE LIKED **ME** EVEN BETTER!

SCHULZ

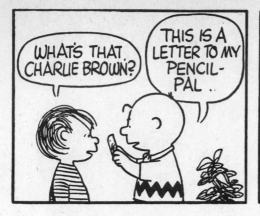

WITH CHARLIE BROWN, FLYING A KITE IS AN EMOTIONAL EXPERIENCE

THUMP

I THINK I'VE FOUND A GOOD MAN FOR SHORTSTOP!

A PITCHER AND HIS CATCHER NEED A GOOD SET OF SIGNALS...

ONE FINGER WILL MEAN A HIGH BALL...

TWO FINGERS WILL MEAN A LOW BALL...

AND THREE FINGERS WILL MEAN THE BROAD AREA IN-BETWEEN!

I PUT MY TOOTH UNDER MY PILLOW LAST NIGHT, BUT ALL I GOT FOR IT WAS A DIME..

THAT'S NOT VERY MUCH, IS IT?

I'LL SAY IT ISN'T. NOT THESE DAYS...

STILL, I SUPPOSE I SHOULDN'T COMPLAIN..

AFTER ALL, THEY DON'T BRING A **THING** ON THE **OPEN MARKET**!

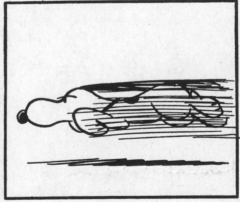

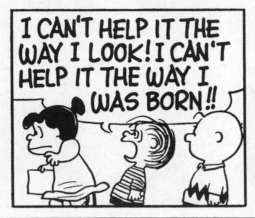

WELL, I JUST LEARNED SOMETHING, CHARLIE BROWN..

NEVER JUMP INTO A PILE OF LEAVES HOLDING A WET SUCKER!

'PIG-PEN,' JUST LOOK AT YOU! YOU'RE A DISGRACE! WHY, YOU'RE A..

STOP RIGHT THERE! BE CAREFUL WHAT YOU SAY!

REMEMBER, THIS SOIL AND I ARE AS ONE..

WHEN YOU CRITICIZE ME, YOU CRITICIZE THE SOIL ON WHICH YOU STAND!

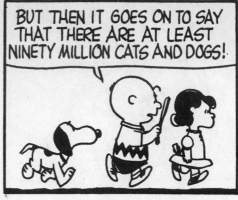

"PIG-PEN" IS THE ONLY PERSON I KNOW WHO CAN GET DIRTY WALKING IN A SNOWSTORM!

PEOPLE LIVE DIFFERENTLY, YOU KNOW..

SOME PEOPLE LIVE IN VERY LARGE HOUSES.. OTHERS LIVE IN ONLY VERY SMALL HOUSES..

LOTS OF PEOPLE EAT AND SLEEP IN THE SAME ROOM..

BLAH

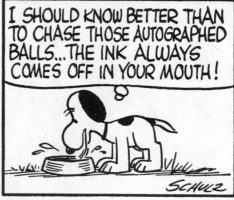

I SHOULD KNOW BETTER THAN TO CHASE THOSE AUTOGRAPHED BALLS...THE INK ALWAYS COMES OFF IN YOUR MOUTH!

SCHULZ

"TOGETHER THEY RODE AWAY ON HIS BIG WHITE HORSE.."

"..AND THEY LIVED HAPPILY EVER AFTER."

SIGH

CONSIDERING ALL THEY WENT THROUGH, I THINK THEY DESERVED A LITTLE HAPPINESS..

SCHULZ

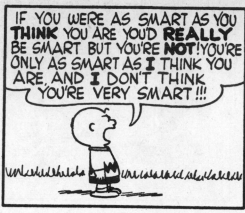

DEAR PENCIL-PAL, I THOUGHT YOU MIGHT BE INTERESTED IN HEARING ABOUT MY FAMILY.

MY DAD IS A BARBER. MY MOTHER IS A HOUSEWIFE.

OH, YES, I ALSO HAVE A DOG NAMED SNOOPY. HE'S KIND OF CRAZY.

I WISH I HAD A PENCIL-PAL LIKE YOU, CHARLIE BROWN..

WELL, IT DOESN'T DO MUCH GOOD IF YOU CAN'T READ NOR WRITE..

THAT'S VERY TRUE...

ONLY FIVE YEARS OLD AND ALREADY I'M ILLITERATE!

SCHULZ